BRICK DAD

HENRY PINTO & CADE FRANKLIN

hachette
AUSTRALIA

Published in Australia and New Zealand in 2021
by Hachette Australia
(an imprint of Hachette Australia Pty Limited)
Level 17, 207 Kent Street, Sydney NSW 2000
www.hachette.com.au

10 9 8 7 6 5 4 3 2 1

 A catalogue record for this
book is available from the
National Library of Australia

ISBN: 978 0 7336 4536 5 (hardback)

Cover design by Luke Causby/Blue Cork
Author photographs and internal photographs courtesy of Channel Nine
Typesetting and internal design by Luke Jensen
Printed and bound in China by 1010 Printing International

ATTENTIVE PARENTING

I HAVE TO TAKE THIS

BEDTIME SHENANIGANS

THE ESCAPE ARTIST

FOLLOWING INSTRUCTION

MUM'S HOME

SIBLING RIVALRY

HOUSE RULES

HOSTILE NEGOTIATIONS

ARE WE THERE YET?

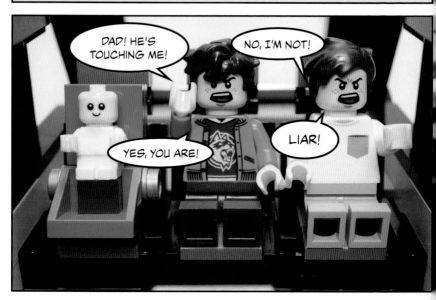

DAD VISION

ARACHNOPHOBIA

MORE BEDTIME SHENANIGANS

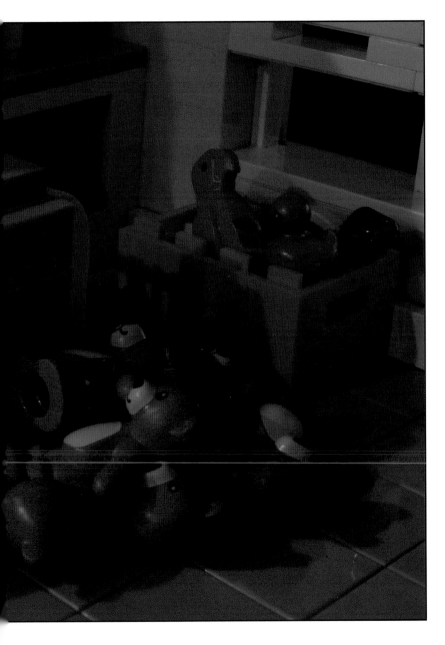

GRAND DESIGNS

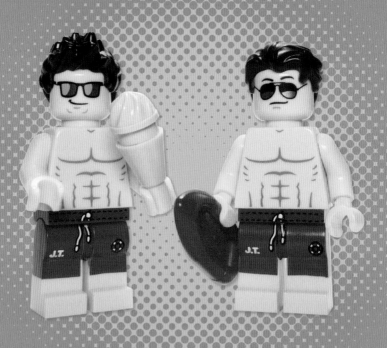

BENDING THE RULES

MULTITASKING

POOL PARTY

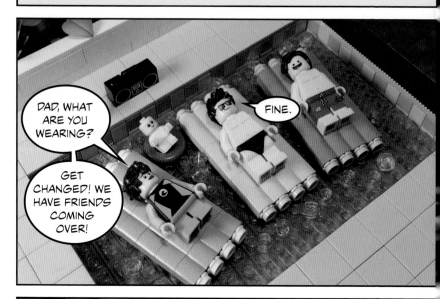

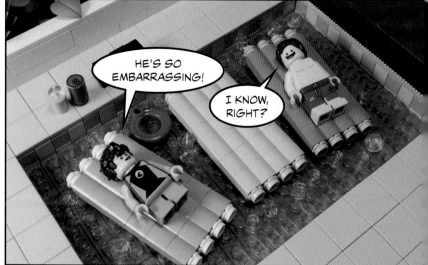

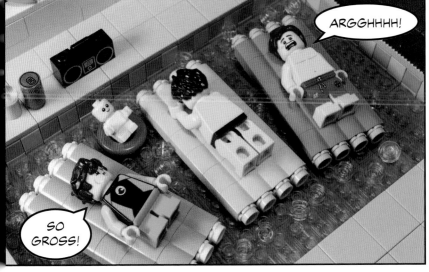

TARGET PRACTICE

BLUE IS MY FAVOURITE COLOUR

SCREEN TIME

SURVIVAL OF THE FITTEST

EVOLUTION EXHIBIT

#TEAMWORK

FAVOURITE SHIRT

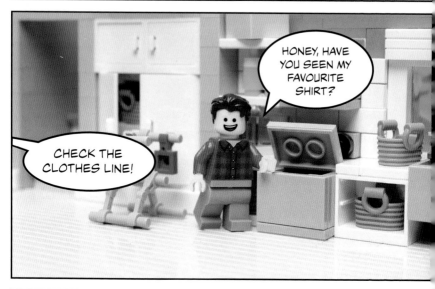

WHAT GOES AROUND COMES AROUND

PACKING LIGHT

'THE TALK'

DADDY'S BOY

SETTING A GOOD EXAMPLE

LIKE FATHER, LIKE SON

BABY'S CHRISTMAS

THANKS, SANTA.

BROTHER'S CHRISTMAS

MORE SIBLING RIVALRY

BOYS NIGHT OUT